PIETER BRUEGEL THE ELDER

T&J

Published by TAJ Books International LLC 2014
5501 Kincross Lane
Charlotte, North Carolina, USA
28277

www.tajbooks.com
www.tajminibooks.com

ISBN 978-1-84406-254-6

Printed in China

1 2 3 4 5 18 17 16 15 14

PIETER BRUEGEL THE ELDER

T&J

SANDRA FORTY

PIETER BRUEGEL THE ELDER

c. 1525–1569

The Flemish artist Pieter Bruegel—sometimes called Peasant Bruegel, and usually distinguished from the other painters in his family as Pieter Bruegel the Elder—was one of the greatest painters of the late medieval/early Renaissance period, whose *The Hunters in the Snow* and *The Peasant Wedding* are as accessible to a modern audience as they were some 500 years ago when he painted them.

Bruegel was the first great artist to paint scenes of ordinary peasant life and show the common man and woman as they went about their daily tasks and amusements. He is credited with bringing a humanizing spirit to painting—something that was lacking in medieval works and entirely absent from contemporary Renaissance paintings. His compositions are full of rich details and reward close examination; in fact, they are used by cultural historians as source material for old Flemish customs, styles of dress, cultivation, and many other aspects of sixteenth-century everyday life.

Pieter Bruegel the Elder was the father of three further generations of artists, most notably his sons—Pieter Brueghel the Younger and Jan Brueghel the Elder—and his grandson, Jan Brueghel the Younger, son of Jan Brueghel the Elder. There were other artists in the family, not least of which was Bruegel's mother-in-law, Mayken Verhulst, a noted watercolorist who was acclaimed as one of the four best female artists of the time.

Pieter Bruegel the Elder spent his working life in Antwerp and Brussels in what was called the Low Countries, now Belgium and the Netherlands. Both cities were important trading ports and economic centers, and Antwerp was the main center of publishing in the Netherlands. The period in which he lived, the mid-1500s, was a turbulent time in history when the Low Countries were occupied by the Catholic Spanish Hapsburgs. Bruegel was born a few years after Martin Luther launched the Protestant Revolution, which initiated much agitation between the Roman Catholic Church and the Protestant Church. Bruegel, who for the period in which he lived made relatively few religious paintings, was not obviously religious.

When Bruegel began to paint, Italian Mannerism was the prevailing style. Initially, however, Bruegel deliberately reverted to the traditional late-Gothic style as exemplified by the Dutch artist Hieronymus Bosch, who although he had died in 1516 was still fashionable and popular in the Low Countries. For a period, Bruegel was even known as "the second Bosch."

Believed to be a self-portrait, c. 1565

Unfortunately, little detail is known about Bruegel's life. The odd legal paper dates him to time and place, and his later paintings are very usefully dated, but much of the personal detail about him has to be inferred. He followed a profession that most considered skilled but artisanal, and therefore unworthy of special attention. He appears to have been something of an intellectual and was a noted humanist, who counted many scholars among his friends, but he did not leave any writings that could have thrown light on his thoughts.

The influence of Hieronymous Bosch and elements of his style persist in Bruegel's compositions until around the early 1560s. Bruegel did bring Bosch's hellish themes up to date by incorporating modern landscapes into the backgrounds as well as contemporary costumes combined with an altogether brighter palette using more structured and refined composition. His early works, although not overtly religious, worked the themes of good and evil, foolish and sinful, usually represented in allegorical form. With maturity, his paintings became more confidently contemporary and secular, showing eloquent commentaries on Flemish peasant life. On close inspection his paintings always carry a moral, and he uses symbols such as peacock feathers to convey vanity.

Bruegel was one of an elite group of intellectuals who pioneered humanist ideas in the Low Countries during the mid-sixteenth century and counted among his friends and patrons many of the leading intellectual lights of the age, including the scholar and cartographer Abraham Ortelius and the important Antwerp printer Christoph Plantin. During his lifetime Bruegel had two principal patrons, the rich Antwerp merchant Nicolaas Jonghelinck and Cardinal Granvelle, although the latter is only known to have owned *Landscape with the Flight into Egypt*. His friend Ortelius also possessed a number of his works, but only his ownership of the *grisaille* (oil) titled *The Dormition of the Virgin* is known for certain.

In the light of the hostile Spanish occupation of the Low Countries, Bruegel had to be very careful not to openly criticize Spain for fear of emphatic retribution, so he hid his opinions within his paintings for viewers to interpret. For example, his *Massacre of the Innocents*, painted about 1566, was an apparently religious piece, but it was actually a criticism of the cruelties and atrocities of the Spanish Inquisition across the Low Countries, as evidenced by the contemporary Flemish village setting.

Bruegel was not interested in painting portraits of the rich and famous, or nudes, or classical scenes from antiquity. Instead, he was interested in everyday peasant life, in how ordinary people worked and passed their leisure time. He is credited with humanizing traditional subjects and personalizing them in a way that had not been attempted before. His only interest in landscapes was as a background for his peasant scenes. These scenes were not idealized, but were composed of people with realistic, coarse faces and dumpy, workmanlike figures. Bruegel was not a peasant himself, but he obviously enjoyed mixing with peasants and learning their routines and lifestyles and was the first painter to depict ordinary peasant life without sentimentalizing or sensationalizing it.

Karel van Mander, Bruegel's Dutch biographer, writing in 1604 identified Brueghel (a location on the present day Dutch–Belgian border) as the artist's birthplace, sometime between 1525 and 1530. The other primary source of information about Bruegel is his contemporary, the Italian writer Guicciardini. Guicciardini names Pieter Bruegel the Elder's birthplace as the nearby town of Breda, in the Duchy of Brabant, which is now in the Netherlands. The latter is the most likely location of Bruegel's birth because he is believed to have been a well-educated townsman rather than a peasant, however, an ancestor of his may have originated in Brueghel.

Bruegel moved to Antwerp, the center of the Flemish publishing world, when he was a young man. Around 1545 he appears to have been apprenticed to Pieter Coecke van Aelst, a successful and greatly admired Flemish painter, architect, sculptor, and designer who worked in the Romanist style and had become court painter to the Holy Roman Emperor Charles V in 1534. Another early artistic influence was the Brunswick Monogrammist, an anonymous Dutch painter who preferred rowdy peasant scenes and religious compositions. The Brunswick Monogrammist is now thought to have been Jan van Amstel, who was related through marriage to Pieter Coecke van Aelst, and therefore would have been known to the young Bruegel and possibly even have tutored him.

By September 1550, Bruegel had left Antwerp and was working in nearby Mechelen in the studio of Claude Dorizi and assisting Peeter Baltens on an altarpiece for the glovemakers guild. The work has not survived, but it is believed that Bruegel worked on the grisaille wings while Baltens worked on the central panel. By October of the following year, Bruegel had qualified as a master in the Guild of Saint Luke and set out for Italy, the land of painting, probably accompanied by the painter Maarten de Vos. From references in letters it seems they went south to France then eastward to Lyon and then by way of Mont Cenis Pass in Savoie through to Susa in Italy. They first went to Bologna, then to Rome before journeying south to Calabria and then to Messina and maybe even Palermo in Sicily and back up to Naples. Their itinerary has been inferred from a variety of third-person letters and copies of drawings attributed to Bruegel.

Bruegel's earliest-dated works are drawings from 1552, *Mountain Landscape with Italian-Style Cloister* and *River Valley with Mountain in the Background*, soon followed by *Harbor at Naples*. By 1553 he was back in Rome where he met the miniaturist Giulio Clovio, who was El Greco's greatest advocate and supporter. In 1587, Clovio's will listed five Bruegels, three of which were landscapes, but unfortunately they have long since disappeared. This is also the time of his earliest-known painting, *Landscape with Christ Appearing to the Apostles at the Sea of Tiberius*, although the figures may have been painted by his traveling companion Maarten de Vos.

It is possible that Bruegel also went to Venice where Titian, an artist he greatly admired, was living and working, but no evidence has ever been found to support this. Nevertheless, he was certainly influenced by Titian.

Sometime in 1554, Bruegel set out for home and was back in Antwerp a year later. Judging by the nonspecific mountain landscape sketches and studies he produced, he journeyed back through the Alps. None of his Alpine vistas can be located geographically, but he made use of them later as composite backgrounds for his paintings.

Antwerp was a busy, flourishing city with an educated, wealthy merchant class that liked to purchase the latest prints for their homes. The city also had a flourishing intellectual scene that attracted many of the great humanists of the time. Many of these people, such as the eminent publisher Christoph Plantin and the great cartographer Ortelius, became close and supportive friends of Bruegel, who was clearly not outclassed by such intellectuals.

In 1555 Bruegel found employment as an engraving designer for Hieronymus Cock, the owner of the Antwerp publishing house At the Four Winds. Known for producing fine prints across a wide range of popular subjects, from landscapes to religious images, Cock was a pioneering print publisher who used specialist craftsmen for the various stages of print and book production. Bruegel became his preferred artist and initially produced landscapes for him. That first year Cock published *Large Landscapes in 12 Prints*, which Bruegel almost certainly worked on but did not sign.

Bruegel quickly appears to have become Cock's preferred artist for allegorical drawings as popular demand soared for moralizing inspiration. Bruegel responded by producing lively pictures full of humor and movement, and stuffed with symbolism for those who wanted to find it. The settings became familiar Flemish villages, and the peasants themselves started to come to the fore in his work.

One of his first published engravings depicted an ancient Latin proverb and was entitled *Big Fish Eat Little Fish*, showing a huge beached fish spewing numerous small fish. It was published by Cock and attributed to Bosch because he was much more saleable than Bruegel. A preliminary drawing of the etching signed by Bruegel and dated 1556 survives, and it may be that he had copied a lost Bosch for the composition. Two years later, however, Bruegel was sufficiently recognized to have his name attached to a hugely detailed series of prints entitled *The Seven Deadly Sins*, or *The Seven Cardinal Vices,* showing an imaginary world full of moral decay, albeit drawing heavily from Bosch's style and approach.

For each of the vices Bruegel showed a personification of the sin in the center foreground, accompanied by a symbolic animal, with the whole surrounded by other aspects of the vice. Each has a Latin inscription identifying the subject: Ira (anger) with a bear; Desidia (sloth) with an ass; Superbia (pride) with a peacock; Avaritia (greed) with a poisonous toad; Gula (gluttony) with a pig; Invidia (envy) with a turkey; and Luxuria (lust) with a lecherous cockerel.

The series must have been popular because he followed it the next year with *The Seven Virtues*, but this time the prints showed a mixture of religious and moral scenes in contemporary Flemish settings including Faith, Hope, and Charity (the Theological Virtues) and Justice, Temperance, Fortitude, and Prudence (the Cardinal Virtues).

Around 1559, Bruegel produced his first signed and dated painting, *Fight Between Carnival and Lent*, which depicted the church on the right and the inn on the left with revelers in between, an allegorical work detailing the fools and sinners of the world. Although still paying homage to Bosch's forms, this painting went in a new direction, having brighter colors and a new compositional approach to groups of figures. Together with two further paintings, *Netherlandish Proverbs* and *Children's Games*, it is considered one of Bruegel's early "encyclopedic" works. Until this point in his career, he had signed his works Brueghel, but in 1559 he dropped the "h" and began signing his paintings and etchings as BRVEGEL.

In 1563 Bruegel painted one of his most famous works, *The Tower of Babel,* for the first time; during his lifetime, he painted the subject three times, twice on wood panels and once, now lost, on ivory. Around this period he also started signing his works with dates in Roman numerals. Called a figurative allegory, *The Tower of Babel* tells a story from the Old Testament, Genesis 11:1–9. It shows a vast, lurching tower with the modern world of Antwerp to the left and the blue sea to the right and in the distance the receding landscape of farms and forests. The theme is the futility of human ambition and commercial greed. With something of the look of the Colosseum in Rome (which he in all probability studied and painted while he was there), Bruegel's tower exudes a schizophrenic aura of disorganized endeavour. The people are dwarfed by the colossal building as they scurry about trying to build the great tower "unto heaven." Close inspection reveals hundreds of tiny people swarming over the vast building like ants, but in uncoordinated effort. The painting is interpreted as a subtle commentary on the occupying Spanish soldiers of Philip II, a swipe at Antwerp's ambitious and avaricious merchants, and a blast at the Roman Catholic Church as supporting the people's greed as long as the church received its share of the bounty. It is unknown whether the painting was commissioned, but by 1566 it belonged to the wealthy Antwerp merchant Nicolaas Jonghelinck.

In late 1563, Bruegel moved to Brussels and in October he married Mayken (aka Maria), the 18-year-old youngest daughter of his old master Pieter Coecke and his second wife, Mayken Verhulst, an illuminator and watercolorist. In Brussels in 1564, Bruegel took a major step toward being a great artist with *The Procession to Calvary*, one of his very few surviving overtly religious works. For the first time he concentrated on creating an atmospheric perspective for which he brought the horizon much lower into the composition.

The years after 1565 are regarded as being Bruegel's mature period, when he was in full command of subject, composition, figures, and landscape. For the next four years until his death he produced many of his greatest paintings. First was a series of six paintings called *The Seasons* commissioned as a frieze to decorate a room for his patron Nicolaas Jonghelinck's house in Antwerp. Today only five of the six survive. The works probably took Bruegel about a year to complete and are a rich combination of figures inhabiting their landscape and showing the cyclical changes of the seasons and the annual cycle of peasant life. Early spring is *The Dark Day* (or *The Gloomy Day*), summer is represented by the *Hay Harvest* (or *Haymaking*), and fall by *The Harvesters*. Perhaps the most celebrated panel is that depicting late fall, called *The Return of the Herd*. The most famous painting in the series is *Hunters in the Snow*, which represents winter. The pictures show the changes on the landscape as the seasons pass and Bruegel adds an extra dimension by changing the predominant color on each panel to match the season. Thus, early spring is mainly brown-

Summer, 1568, Kunsthalle Hamburg,
22 x 28.6 cm, Pen and India ink

black, spring (the missing panel) would have been blue, haymaking green, harvesting corn yellow, fall mustard yellow, and winter white with snow.

Unfortunately, after only owning them for a few months, Jonghelinck used them—as well as other Bruegels, 22 works by Frans Floris, and a Dürer—as surety against a debt of 16,000 guilders on which he defaulted. The paintings were forfeited and disappeared until the city of Antwerp presented them to the governor of the Spanish Netherlands, Archduke Ernst, in 1594.

Despite the ambitious scope of the six panels in *The Seasons*, Bruegel also had time to revisit former fields. Around this time he painted a second version of *The Tower of Babel* and his son Pieter (later known as Pieter Brueghel the Younger) was born.

Bruegel populated his paintings with bustling people in animated detail, living life to the full. He completed *The Peasant Dance* around 1567, which shows ordinary people eating, drinking, dancing, and talking. But the work also shows the moral frailties with which people are plagued, such as excessive drinking, anger, and pride. Its companion piece, *The Peasant Wedding Feast*, dates from the same time and provides an invaluable social record of how such a celebration was arranged. The feast takes place on the threshing room floor, where slightly right of center and in front of a canopy, sits the bride wearing a wreath.

Traditionally, she would not do any work on her wedding day, the only day in her hard life when she could truly rest. Her groom, according to custom, was not allowed to sit at the table and may even be the man Bruegel painted serving beer.

In 1566, Bruegel returned to engraving and etching and the following year he produced a drawing called *The Artist and the Connoisseur* showing two half-length figures. The heavily eyebrowed and rather glum bearded artist is generally supposed to be a self-portrait. Another perhaps more likely, although also disputed, self-portrait appears on the extreme right in *The Procession to Calvary*.

In 1567, Bruegel's second son, Jan Brueghel, was born and at some point in their marriage the Bruegels also had a daughter, but nothing is known about her except that, like her brothers, she was born in Brussels. Jan and Pieter may have been taught to paint with watercolors by their grandmother Mayken.

Bruegel's last painting was probably *Magpie on the Gallows,* which shows three peasants dancing in a woodland clearing while a magpie looks on from its perch on a gallows. During the year, the Duke of Alba had mercilessly scourged the Netherlands to suppress the Dutch Revolt and stamp out Protestantism. The gallows in the painting are a symbol of repression and the magpie represents the danger of gossiping, which in turn could lead to hanging. A second magpie sits on a tree stump at the base of the gallows. A Flemish proverb of the time talks of "shitting" on the gallows, which is interpreted as mocking the state, and in the shadows in the extreme left foreground a man is doing just that.

On September 5, 1569, Bruegel died. His old friend Ortelius described him in print as "the most perfect painter of his time." He reportedly ordered his wife to burn a number of his works that he thought might present a danger to her. Perhaps he believed they were too critical of the Spanish occupation and rule in the Low Countries. He told her to keep *Magpie on the Gallows* for herself.

Bruegel undoubtedly painted many more works but they have disappeared over the centuries. Most of his surviving 40 paintings date from a 12-year period from 1557 to his death in 1569, and almost two-thirds of those from the last six years when he lived in Brussels. A third of his paintings are held by the Kunsthistorisches Museum in Vienna as a result of the Imperial Hapsburg collectors Archduke Ernst and Emperor Rudolf II. He also left around 61 attributed drawings. Many signed drawings dating between 1559 and 1562 once thought to be by Bruegel have been reattributed to Jacques Savery and Roelandt Savery, who may or may not have been trying to pass them off as originals.

Bruegel's legacy was ensured not just through his work but also through his direct line, both his sons—Pieter Brueghel the Younger and Jan Brueghel the Elder, they both kept the "h" in their name—went on to become celebrated painters in their own right, though neither of them quite shared the genius of their father. Succeeding generations of Dutch and Flemish genre and landscape painters took inspiration from Pieter Bruegel the Elder, none less so than the great Peter Paul Rubens. But apart from his immediate compatriots, for the next three hundred years Bruegel's paintings were largely dismissed as nothing more than bucolic caricatures. Many of his paintings disappeared into the Hapsburg collection, which possessed 14 works, and other elite collections away from public view. Much of his known works were only in the form of engravings and crude copies. Pieter Bruegel the Elder's exceptional eye and artistic skill were only reassessed at the start of the 20th century, but since then his greatness has been assured and his paintings have emerged in public collections for all to see.

Because many of Bruegel's works are engravings, multiple prints of the same engraving exist and are in the collections of more than one museum. *The Seven Deadly Sins* and *The Seven Virtues* series are examples of this. Whereas only one provenance is given in the book, it is not exhaustive.

Plate 1

LANDSCAPE WITH CHRIST APPEARING TO THE APOSTLES AT THE SEA OF TIBERIUS

1553, Private Collection

THE ADORATION OF THE KINGS

Plate 2

1556-62, Musees Royaux des Beaux-Arts de Belgique, Brussels
122 x 168 cm, Tempera on canvas

Plate 3

THE ASS IN THE SCHOOL
1556, National Museums, Berlin
23 x 30 cm, Pen and ink

BIG FISH EAT LITTLE FISH

1557, The Metropolitan Museum of Art, New York City
22.9 x 29.6 cm, Engraving

Plate 4

GRANDIBVS EXIGVI SVNT PISCES PISCIBVS ESCA.
Siet sone dit hebbe ick zeer langhe gheweten / dat die groote vissen de cleyne eten

Plate 5

PARABLE OF THE SOWER
1557, Timken Museum of Art, San Diego
73.7 x 102.9 cm, Oil on panel

THE ADORATION OF THE KINGS IN THE SNOW

1557, Oskar Reinhart Foundation, Winterthur, Switzerland
35 x 55 cm, Wood panel

Plate 6

Plate 7

THE FALL OF ICARUS

1558, Musees Royaux des Beaux-Arts de Belgique, Brussels
73 x 112 cm, Oil on canvas

Plate 8

DETAIL: THE FALL OF ICARUS

Plate 9

BATTLE OFF THE PORT OF NAPLES
c. 1558, Galleria Doria Pamphilj, Rome
41 x 70 cm, Oil on panel

Plate 10

DETAIL: BATTLE OFF THE PORT OF NAPLES

Plate 11

TWELVE PROVERBS ON WOODEN PLATES
1558, Museum Mayer van den Bergh, Antwerp, Belgium
74.5 x 98.4 cm, Oak

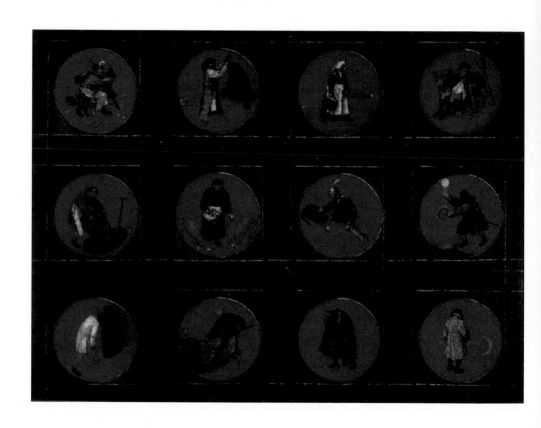

SLOTH (DESIDIA)
FROM THE SEVEN DEADLY SINS SERIES

Plate 12

1558, The Metropolitan Museum of Art, New York City
22.5 x 29.2 cm, Engraving

Plate 13

GREED (AVARITIA)
FROM THE SEVEN DEADLY SINS SERIES

1558, The Metropolitan Museum of Art, New York City
22.5 x 29.2 cm, Engraving

Plate 14

LUST (LUXURIA)
FROM THE SEVEN DEADLY SINS SERIES
1558, Museum Boijmans, Rotterdam, Netherlands
21.2 x 29.5 cm, Engraving

Plate 15

PRIDE (SUPERBIA)
FROM THE SEVEN DEADLY SINS SERIES

1558, British Museum, London
22.6 x 29.3 cm, Engraving

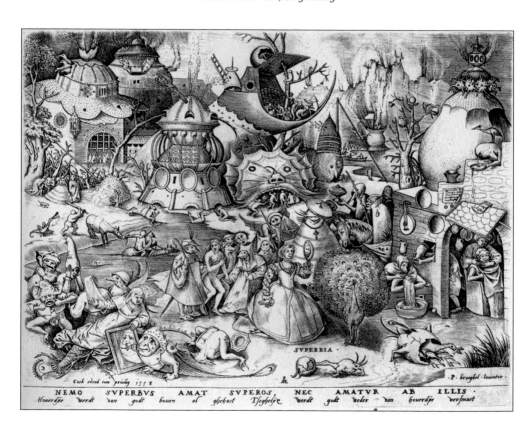

SVPERBIA ·

NEMO SVPERBVS AMAT SVPEROS, NEC AMATVR AB ILLIS.

Plate 16

GLUTTONY (GULA)
FROM THE SEVEN DEADLY SINS SERIES
1558, British Museum, London
22.3 x 29.4 cm, Engraving

GVLA·

EBRIETAS EST VITANDA INGLVVIESQVE CIBORVM.

Plate 17

ANGER (IRA)
FROM THE SEVEN DEADLY SINS SERIES
1558, The Metropolitan Museum of Art, New York City
22.5 x 29.7 cm, Engraving

· P. brueghel · Inventor ·   IRA   · H · Cock · edendo · Cum gratia et privilegio · 1 5 5 8 ·

ORA   TVMENT   IRA,   NIGRESCVNT   SANGVINE   VENÆ.
Gramscap doet den mont swillen / en verbittert den moet   Sŷ beroert den gheest / en maeckt swert dat bloet

Plate 18

ENVY (INVIDIA)
FROM THE SEVEN DEADLY SINS SERIES
1558, The Metropolitan Museum of Art, New York City
22.7 x 29.5 cm, Engraving

INVIDIA HORRENDVM MONSTRVM, SÆVISSIMA PESTIS
Een onsterffelijcke doot es nijt en wreede peste Een beost die haer seluen eet met valschen moleste

Plate 19

FIGHT BETWEEN CARNIVAL AND LENT

1559, Kunsthistorisches Museum, Vienna
118 x 165 cm, Oil on panel

Plate 20

DETAIL: FIGHT BETWEEN CARNIVAL AND LENT

Plate 21

NETHERLANDISH PROVERBS
1559, National Museums, Berlin
117 x 163 cm, Oil on board

Plate 22

Plate 23

CHARITY (CHARITAS)
FROM THE SEVEN VIRTUES SERIES

c. 1559, Museum of Fine Arts Boston
22.5 x 29 cm, Engraving

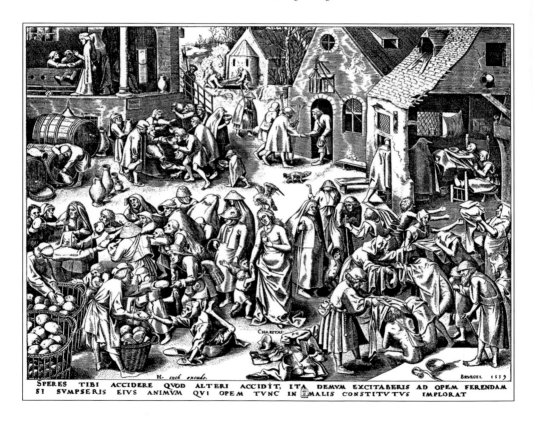

SPERES TIBI ACCIDERE QVOD ALTERI ACCIDIT, ITA DEMVM EXCITABERIS AD OPEM FERENDAM
SI SVMPSERIS EIVS ANIMVM QVI OPEM TVNC IN MALIS CONSTITVTVS IMPLORAT

FAITH (FIDES)
FROM THE SEVEN VIRTUES SERIES
c. 1559-60, The Metropolitan Museum of Art, New York City
24.2 x 30.2 cm, Engraving

FIDES MAXIMÈ À NOBIS CONSERVANDA EST RRAECIPVE IN RELIGIONEM, QVIA DEVS PRIOR ET POTÉNTIOR EST QVAM HOMO.

37

Plate 25

FORTITUDE (FORTITUDO)
FROM THE SEVEN VIRTUES SERIES

c. 1560, Museum of Fine Arts Boston
22 x 28.8 cm, Engraving

FORTITVDO

ANIMVM VINCERE, IRACVNDIAM COHIBERE CAETERAQ VITIA ET AFFECTVS
COHIBERE VERA FORTITVDO EST·

Plate 26

HOPE (SPES)
FROM THE SEVEN VIRTUES SERIES

c. 1559, Museum of Fine Arts Boston
22.6 x 29.1 cm, Engraving

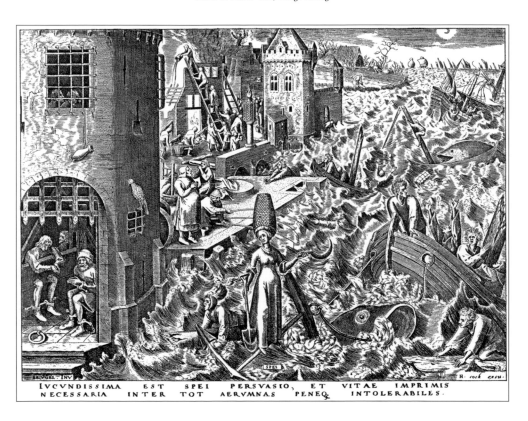

IVCVNDISSIMA EST SPEI PERSVASIO, ET VITAE IMPRIMIS NECESSARIA INTER TOT AERVMNAS PENEQ INTOLERABILES.

Plate 27

JUSTICE (JUSTICIA)
FROM THE SEVEN VIRTUES SERIES
c. 1559, Museum of Fine Arts Boston
22.2 x 29 cm, Engraving

SCOPVS LEGIS EST, AVT VT EV̄ QVE PVNIT EMENDET, AVT POENA EIVS CAETEROS MELIORES REDDET AVT SVBLATIS MALIS CAETERI SECVRIORES VIVAT̄.

Plate 28

PRUDENCE (PRUDENCIA)
FROM THE SEVEN VIRTUES SERIES

c. 1559, Museum of Fine Arts Boston
22.4 x 29.7 cm, Engraving

PRUDENTIA

SI PRVDENS ESSE CVPIS, IN FVTVRVM PROSPECTVM OSTENDE, ET
QVAE POSSVNT CONTINGERE, ANIMO TVO CVNCTA PROPONE

Plate 29

TEMPERANCE (TEMPERANTIA)
FROM THE SEVEN VIRTUES SERIES

c. 1560, Museum of Fine Arts Boston
22.5 x 29 cm, Engraving

VIDENDVM, VT NEC VOLVPTATI DEDITI PRODIGI ET LVXVRIOSI
APPAREAMVS, NEC AVARA TENACITATI SORDIDI AVT OBCVRI EXISTAMVS

Plate 30

THE FAIR OF SAINT GEORGE'S DAY

c. 1559-1610, Museum of Fine Arts, Houston

33.6 x 52.4 cm

Plate 31

CHILDREN'S GAMES
1560, Kunsthistorisches Museum, Vienna
118 x 161 cm, Oil

Plate 33

THE RABBIT HUNT
1560, Museum of Fine Arts Boston
22.2 x 22.9 cm, Etching

Plate 34

MAD MEG

1562, Museum Mayer van den Bergh, Antwerp, Belgium
117.4 x 162 cm, Oil on canvas

Plate 35

FALL OF REBEL ANGELS

1562, Musees Royaux des Beaux-Arts de Belgique, Brussels
117 x 162 cm, Oil on board

Plate 36

DETAIL: FALL OF REBEL ANGELS

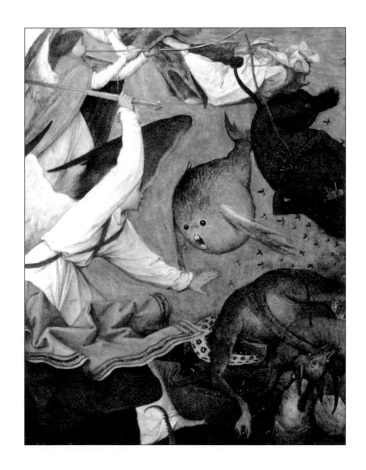

Plate 37

THE SUICIDE OF SAUL
1562, Kunsthistorisches Museum, Vienna
34 x 55 cm, Oil on panel

Plate 38

DETAIL: THE SUICIDE OF SAUL

Plate 39

TWO MONKEYS
1562, National Museums, Berlin
20 x 23 cm, Oil on panel

POTRAIT OF AN OLD WOMAN
1563, Alte Pinakothek, Munich
22 x 18 cm, Oil on wood panel

Plate 40

Plate 41

THE TRIUMPH OF DEATH

c. 1562, Museo del Prado, Madrid
117 x 162 cm, Oil on panel

Plate 43

LANDSCAPE WITH THE FLIGHT INTO EGYPT

1563, The Courtauld Institute of Art, London
37.1 x 55.6 cm, Oil on panel

Plate 44

THE TOWER OF BABEL
1563, Kunsthistorisches Museum, Vienna
114 x 155 cm, Oil on canvas

THE TOWER OF BABEL

Plate 45

c. 1565, Museum Boijmans, Rotterdam, Netherlands
59.9 x 74.6 cm, Oil on panel

Plate 46

THE PROCESSION·TO CALVARY
1564, Kunsthistorisches Museum, Vienna
124 x 170 cm, Oil on canvas

Plate 48
CHRIST AND THE WOMAN TAKEN IN ADULTERY

1565, The Courtauld Institute of Art, London
24.1 x 34.4 cm, Oil on panel

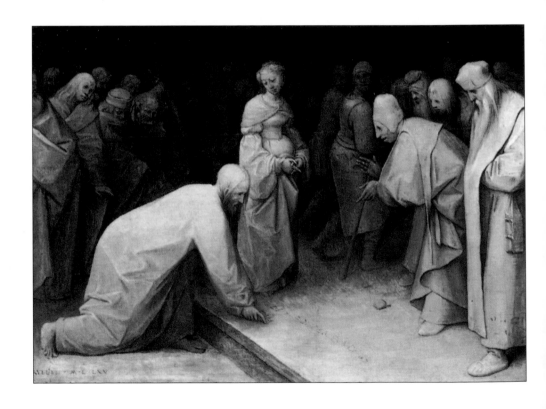

THE DORMITION OF THE VIRGIN

c. 1564, National Trust, Upton House, Banbury, England
37 x 55.5 cm, Oil on oak panel

Plate 49

Plate 50

THE GLOOMY DAY
1565, Kunsthistorisches Museum, Vienna
118 x 163 cm, Oil on canvas

Plate 51

HAYMAKING
1565, Lobkowicz Palace, Prague, Czech Republic
161 x 117 cm, Oil on wood panel

Plate 52

THE HARVESTERS

1565, The Metropolitan Museum of Art, New York City
116.5 x 159.5 cm, Oil on wood

Plate 53

THE RETURN OF THE HERD
1565, Kunsthistorisches Museum, Vienna
117 x 156 cm, Oil on panel

Plate 54

HUNTERS IN THE SNOW

1565, Kunsthistorisches Museum, Vienna
117 x 162 cm, Oil on panel

Plate 55

WINTER LANDSCAPE WITH SKATERS AND A BIRD TRAP

1565, Musees Royaux des Beaux-Arts de Belgique, Brussels
37 x 55 cm, Oil on panel

Plate 56

THE CENSUS AT BETHLEHEM
1566, Musees Royaux des Beaux-Arts de Belgique, Brussels
115.5 x 163.5 cm, Oil on board

Plate 57

Plate 58

THE WEDDING DANCE
c. 1566, Detroit Institute of Arts
119.4 x 157.5 cm, Oil on panel

Plate 59

THE LAND OF COCKAIGNE
1566, Alte Pinakothek, Munich
52 x 78 cm, Wood

Plate 60

MASSACRE OF THE INNOCENTS
c. 1565–67, Royal Collection Trust, United Kingdom
109.2 x 158.1 cm, Oil on panel

Plate 62

THE WINE OF SAINT MARTIN'S DAY

c. 1565-68, Museo del Prado, Madrid
148 x 270.5 cm, Tempera on linen

Plate 63

THE CONVERSION OF SAUL

1567, Kunsthistorisches Museum,
Vienna
108 x 156 cm, Oil on panel

Plate 64

THE PEASANT DANCE

c. 1567, Kunsthistorisches Museum, Vienna
114 x 164 cm, Oil on panel

Plate 65

Plate 66

THE PEASANT WEDDING
1560, Kunsthistorisches Museum, Vienna
114 x 164 cm, Oil on board

Plate 67

DETAIL: THE PEASANT WEDDING

Plate 68

STORM AT SEA
1568, Kunsthistorisches Museum, Vienna
71 x 97 cm, Oil on panel

Plate 69

DETAIL: STORM AT SEA

Plate 70

THE BEGGARS
1568, Musée du Louvre, Paris
18 x 21 cm, Oil on panel